Hello. If I have been silly enough to mislay this diary please return it to:

Mr. Bean
c/o Mrs. Wicket
"Daffodils"
12 Arbor Road
LONDON N10

A £5–00 reward would certainly not be out of the question.

The number of i's on this page is 53
~~53~~
~~56~~
~~57~~
~~61~~

First published in the UK in 1992 by
BOXTREE LIMITED,
Broadwall House,
21 Broadwall,
London SE1 9PL

10 9 8 7 6 5

Text copyright © Tiger Television, 1992
Photographs copyright © Tiger Television, 1992

Designed by Nigel Davies for Titan Studio.
Photography by Paul Forrester.
Reproduced by Positive Colour Ltd.
Printed and bound in Great Britain by
Butler & Tanner Ltd, Frome and London.

A catalogue record for this book is available from the
British Library.

ISBN 1 85283 768 3

my place

Mr. Bean's

HIGHBURY DISTRICT COUNCIL DIARY 1993

so watch it

Compiled for the H.D.C. by
Robin Driscoll and Rowan Atkinson
of the National Diary, Calendar and Phases of the Moon Office
at the Department of National Heritage

B⊞XTREE

HIGHBURY DISTRICT COUNCIL

LIGHT SWITCH

BED

WARDROBE

SHUT UP!

Mayor
Sarah Mahaffy
32 Tongdean Rise,
London N5

Councillor
Nichola Motley
Housing Committee
Broadwaters,
308 Waldergrave Rd,
London N5

Councillor David Inman
Planning Committee
29 Duchland Avenue, London NW8

Councillor Susan Cole
Environment Committee
Flat 3, 21 Downlands Close, London N9

Councillor Chantel Noel
Women's Committee
c/o Highbury Town Hall

Councillor Rod Green
Policy Committee
c/o Highbury Town Hall

MOO

Councillor Adrian Sington
Emergency Committee
Church Villas, 15 Dukes Road, London N5

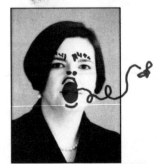

Councillor Elaine Collins
Equal Oportunities Committee
4a George Street, London NW4

Temperature Conversions

°C	°F	°C	°F	°C	°F	°C	°F	°C	°F	°C	°F
-20	-4.0	1	33.8	22	71.6	43	109.4	64	147.2	85	185.0
-19	-2.2	2	35.6	23	73.4	44	111.2	65	149.0	86	186.8
-18	-0.4	3	37.4	24	75.2	45	113.0	66	150.8	87	188.6
-17	1.4	4	39.2	25	77.0	46	114.8	67	152.6	88	190.4
-16	3.2	5	41.0	26	78.8	47	116.6	68	154.4	89	192.2
-15	5.0	6	42.8	27	80.6	48	118.4	69	156.2	90	194.0
-14	6.8	7	44.6	28	82.4	49	120.2	70	158.0	91	195.8
-13	8.6	8	46.4	29	84.2	50	122.0	71	159.8	92	197.6
-12	10.4	9	48.2	30	86.0	51	123.8	72	161.6	93	199.4
-11	12.2	10	50.0	31	87.8	52	125.6	73	163.4	94	201.2
-10	14.0	11	51.8	32	89.6	53	127.4	74	165.2	95	203.0
-9	15.8	12	53.6	33	91.4	54	129.2	75	167.0	96	204.8
-8	17.6	13	55.4	34	93.2	55	131.0	76	168.8	97	206.6
-7	19.4	14	57.2	35	95.0	56	132.8	77	170.6	98	208.4
-6	21.2	15	59.0	36	96.8	57	134.6	78	172.4	99	210.2
-5	23.0	16	60.8	37	98.6	58	136.4	79	174.2	100	212.0
-4	24.8	17	62.6	38	100.4	59	138.2	80	176.0	101	213.8
-3	26.6	18	64.4	39	102.2	60	140.0	81	177.8	102	215.6
-2	28.4	19	66.2	40	104.0	61	141.8	82	179.6	103	217.4
-1	30.2	20	68.0	41	105.8	62	143.6	83	181.4	104	219.2
0	32.0	21	69.8	42	107.6	63	145.4	84	183.2	105	221.0

Conversion Values

Distance

miles to kilometres	1.6093
yards to metres	0.9144
feet to metres	0.3048
inches to millimetres	25.4
inches to centimetres	2.54

Area

square miles to square kilometres	2.59
square miles to hectares	258.99
acres to square metres	4046.86
acres to hectares	0.4047
square yards to square metres	0.8361
square feet to square metres	0.0929
square feet to square centimetres	929.03
square inches to square centimetres	645.16
square inches to square millimetres	6.4516

Volume

cubic yards to cubic metres	0.7646
cubic feet to cubic metres	0.0283
cubic inches to cubic centimetres	16.3871

Capacity

gallons to litres	4.546
quarts to litres	1.137
pints to litres	0.568
gills to litres	0.142

Speed

miles per hour to kilometres per hour	1.6093
feet per second to metres per second	0.3048
feet per minute to metres per second	0.0051
feet per minute to metres per minute	0.3048
inches per second to millimetres per second	25.4
inches per minute to millimetres per second	0.4233
inches per minute to millimetres per minute	2.54

Mass

tons to kilograms	1016.05
tons to tonnes	1.0160
hundredweights to kilograms	50.8023
centals to kilograms	45.3592
quarters to kilograms	12.7006
stones to kilograms	6.3503
pounds to kilograms	0.4536
ounces to grams	28.3495

Mass per Unit Area

tons per square mile to kilograms per square hectare	3.923
pounds per sq. foot to kilograms per sq. metre	4.8824
pounds per sq. inch to grams per sq. centimetre	70.307
ounces per sq. foot to grams per sq. metre	305.152

Mass per Unit Length

tons per mile to kilograms per metre	0.6313
pounds per foot to kilograms per metre	1.4882
pounds per inch to kilograms per metre	17.858
ounces per inch to grams per millimetre	1.1161

Fuel Consumption

gallons per mile to litres per mile	2.825
miles per gallon to kilometres per litre	0.354

Addresses & Telephone Numbers

The Queen
Buckingham Palace (Flat No.?)
London
ENGLAND .... Esc directory

Inspector Morse
Oxford Nick
Oxfordshire 999

~~Mrs Wilson~~
~~Highbury Library~~
~~Highbury~~

Prime Minister
10 Downing Street
London (Weekdays) 071 290 3000

Chequers (W/ends) 0945 482451
(PayPhone — Pub)

Shirley Bassey
On my Wall
~~Eat~~ In my room
My House
My Street
ENGLAND 081 467 8290

~~Mrs Wilkinson~~ KILL KILL
KILL
KILL

GOD
Everywhere

(literally, apparently)

Crematorium
(That place in the trees with
the chimney)

081 858 5010

Mum
Clapham Cemetery

Grandad
~~Grove Road~~
~~London N4~~
(Moved in with Mum)

Shoe Store 071 736 5926

December

Xmas '92

Oooh! Diary for Christmas

3pm Queen

26 Saturday

↑

Boxing Day?

27 Sunday ↗↑↖

??

Still no sign of Boxing Day

December

28 Monday Boxing Day

~~Dear Mrs. Queen~~

~~Dear Eliz~~

Dear The Queen

I hope you are well. I am fine. A most peculiar thing has happened. You may remember that last year Boxing Day was on the day after Christmas, and most properly so. Why oh why ~~oh why~~

Ever since ~~Alexander that man~~

~~Napoleon~~ Bonaparte was never blown apart 👁

11:00 Corner Shop
PILCHARDS

---

29 Tuesday

→ 291 2777

9.00 Hospital

Tell Doctor: Both ends went in the night

Pilchard?

December

30 Wednesday

12.00 Pie in
12.25 Pie out

31 Thursday

Put the slippery soap
On the slippery slope

NEW YEAR
RESOLUTIONS

1. Become millionaire
2. Tidy room.
3. Buy other slipper

27. Marriage

Set alarm for 12.00 midnight

January

1 Friday

A brand spanking New Year
Clean and shiny and
spatkling and lovely

1993 — GLINT

GLEAM

DURA GLIT

SHIRLEY BASSEY
9.00 Ch4 ?!?

10,000 watts

2 Saturday

3 Sunday

January

4 Monday

9.40 Buy new swimming Trunks.

11.00 Try Trunks (POOL)

5 Tuesday

10.00 Report Police Station (re. Trunks
coming off)

(Letter of Apology) TO: St. Bernadette's School for Girls.
Hampstead Road London NW1

Dear ~~Lor~~ Headmistress
Can't apologise enough for awful
incident in front of your young women. ~~~~
~~~~ My ~~~~ ~~~~

4.00 POST BOX

6 Wednes

Dear Mr Bean
Rent when I get
home (Sat).

Mrs Wicket

SWINDON BY NIGHT

Mr Bean c/o Mrs Wicket
'Daffodils'
12 Arbor   Rd
London
N10

1ST

7 Thursday

January

8 Friday

4.00 Bottom Problem

9 Saturday

7.45 Keep Fit with
thin woman (ITV)

9.00   20 Press Ups
20 Sit Ups
20 Pull Ups
20 Jump Ups

10 Sunday

9.00 20 Press Ups
20 Sit Ups
20 Pull Ups
20 Jump Ups

That one with the fat
girl 8.00
BBC2

January

11 Monday

9.00 10 ~~20~~ Press Ups
10 ~~20~~ Sit Ups
10 ~~20~~ Pull Ups
10 ~~20~~ Jump Ups   10.00 LIBRARY

Try ~~to~~ get: "GUNS OF NAVARONE"

"HIS BODY WAS IN BITS"
by Zak Brood

$↓$ CLIFF

"DEATH IS FREQUENTLY UNEXPECTED"
(Z. Brood)

12 Tuesday

9.00 4 ~~20~~ Press Ups
4 ~~20~~ Sit Ups
4 ~~20~~ Pull Ups
4 ~~20~~ Jump Ups

2.30 Go back and peek
at Librarian
(re. Marriage)

Wobble Dobble Fobble Bobble

January

13 Wednesday

9.00   20 PRESS UPS
         20 SIT UPS
         20 PULL UPS
         20 JUMP UPS

10.00 Peek at Librarian

14 Thursday

9.00 20 PRESS UPS
     20 SIT UPS
     20 PULL UPS
     20 JUMP UPS

Irma something

NO NO
NO
NO
NO NO NO
NO
NO 0000000 NO

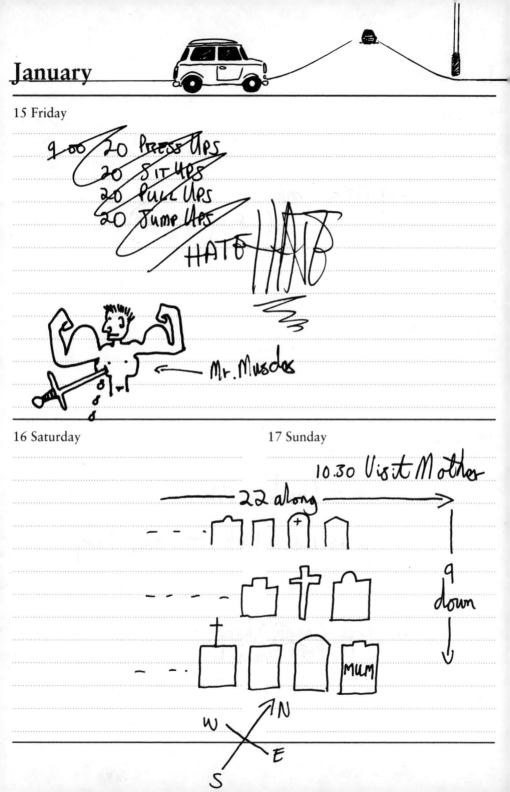

15 Friday

9.00 20 PRESS UPS
20 SIT UPS
20 PULL UPS
20 JUMP UPS

HATE HATE

← Mr. Muscles

16 Saturday

17 Sunday

10.30 Visit Mother

← 22 along →

9 down

MUM

N
W
E
S

January

18 Monday

Ring Irma Gobb

(Library 658 4690)

19 Tuesday

12.15 Lunch in PARK

12.25 Leave Park (Too much Poo)

4.00 Shops: Carpet Shampoo
Pott Pourri

January

20 Wednesday

9.15 Park

STILL too much Poo in Park

DOG DEVICE

CORK

© Mr. Bean

21 Thursday

Ring Inspector Morse

January

22 Friday

Dear Inspector Morse
There's so much poo in our Park you wouldn't believe it. Can you come and investigate?

I will gladly help you. I have a good ~~set~~ set of spanners

Mr. Bee Bee Bean ©

23 Saturday

That loud one with the beard 630 ITV

24 Sunday

Vicar out all day

25 Monday

10.00 Library ♡

Take back : Guns of Nav.
2 x Z. Brood

Take out : "Gone with the Wind" (ROMANCE)

"Stand and Deliver"
(Autobiog. of Mollie Saxton, Midwife)

"His blood ran fredy" by Zak Brood

26 Tuesday

MR. BEAN
invites you to a Party at
The Park (near Coin-Op Toilets)

DISASTER
IF WET

BRING A SANDWICH
(TWO IF YOU'RE FAT)

Send to
Irma

January

27 Wednesday

4.45 Ring Irma Gobb

Put Cat out ~~of its misery~~

28 Thursday

4.45 Ring Gobb

January
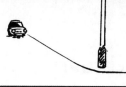

29 Friday

1.30 Wash Spanners

4.45 Get Gobb

30 Saturday

Irma Gobb
Has got a Job
In a busy Library
She does her Job
(Does Irma Gobb)
In a library north of Highbury
Irma Gobb
Who's got this Job
Somewhere north of Highbury
Is the same old Irma Gobb
Whose hands are thin and fibrey

31 Sunday

Stephen Bixley

February

1 Mon

Romance?

8.10 Take Irma Gobbto Pictures

2 Tuesday

Bob a Bob
Joba Bob

Goba Goba Gobble Gobble

February

3 Wednesday

9.00 Ring Gobb

10.00 Ring Gobb

11.00 Ring Gobb

12.00 Ring Gobb

1.00 Ring Gobb

Where is Gobb?

4 Thursday

8.30 Ring Gobb	11.30 Ring Gobb	2.30 Ring Gobb
8.45 Ring Gobb	11.45 Ring Gobb	2.45 Ring Gobb
9.00 Ring Gobb	12.00 Ring Gobb	3.00 Ring Gobb
9.15 Ring Gobb	12.15 Ring Gobb	3.15 Ring Gobb
9.30 Ring Gobb	12.30 Ring Gobb	3.30 Ring Gobb
9.45 Ring Gobb	12.45 Ring Gobb	3.45 Ring Gobb
10.00 Ring Gobb	1.00 Ring Gobb	4.00 Ring Gobb
10.05 Ring Gobb	1.15 Ring Gobb	4.15 Ring Gobb
10.30 Ring Gobb	1.30 Ring Gobb	4.30 Ring Gobb
11.00 Ring Gobb	1.45 Ring Gobb	4.45 Ring Gobb
11.15 Ring Gobb	2.00 Ring Gobb	5.00 Ring Gobb
11.30 Ring Gobb	2.15 Ring Gobb	5.15 Ring Gobb
		6.00 Ring Gobb
		6.15 Ring Gobb
		6.30 Ring Gobb

February

5 Friday

HATE HATE
HATE
HATE
HATE HATE
HATE
HATE HATE
HATE HATE
HATE HATE
HATE

HATE

Dear All,
I am having a lovely holiday in Minorca with ~~friends~~. The weather is delightful and Giles ~~is great fun~~. I hear the weather there is terrible —HOORAY! I will be back at work on the 8th. Lots of love
Irma x

GREETINGS FROM MINORCA

Library
Highbur
Lond
EN

6 Saturday

10.00 Smiths Do-It-All
Either SNIPER RIFLE
OR ROPE
SHEATH KNIFE
STRICHNINE
MOUSETRAP?

7 Sunday

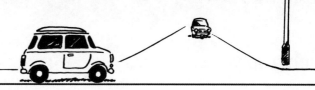

February

8 Monday

Hurt
Flay Rip
Slash Gouge
Hit
Stab

If I put a bomb under Giles
He will go for miles and miles
And miles and miles and miles
and MILES

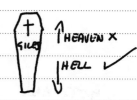

COFFIN (GILES)
↑ HEAVEN X
↓ HELL ✓

9 Tuesday

VENGEANCE

9.30 Crimewatch UK BBC1
(Ideas)

February

10 Wednesday

2.45 Report to
Police Station

Go to bed
zzzzzzzzzzzzzzzz
11 Thursday Wake up

2.00 — 2.10 Sunny

METROPOLITAN POLICE   your ref:
RECEIPT
                          our ref:

Surrendered Goods

1 BRNO .22 AIR RIFLE
1 10" KNIFE
1 SMOKE CANISTOR
3 MOUSE TRAPS
1 lt. ARALDITE
10 m. ROPE

P.C.R. Leavis

The above items have been confiscated pending
a decision by local magistrates

I love P.C. Leavis
x
x x
x

February

12 Friday

Buy Fudge ~~Grow beard~~ NO
                        YES ✓✓✓
                            ✓✓✓

13 Saturday

Roses are red
Violets are blue
You were Miss Gobb
And I was Mr.

~~Goo~~ ~~spew thee Ahoo~~
~~Foo man choo~~
~~What Goo~~
        True ✓

14 Sunday   St Valentine's Day

No card

Samaritans
071 2367925

10.00 Put Out Bin

February

15 Monday

16 Tuesday

February

17 Wednesday

18 Thursday

February

19 Friday

20 Saturday

21 Sunday

February

22 Monday

23 Tuesday

February

24 Wednesday

FOUND DIARY!!

25 Thursday

Hiphip hoozar
Hiphop haha
Yipee Yippee Bippee Bippee

1.15 Soup

HAPPINESS

February

26 Friday

No.3.

Dear Mr Bean,
We havn't met yet but
I have just moved into No3
down the hall. Enclosed is
your diary which I found
today by the bins in the porch.
I would very much like to
call to make your acquaintance
and perhaps to pick up the
reward you mentioned on
the first page?!

Man in
No.3.

Avoid Man in
No.3

27 Saturday

N.B. Man in No.3

N.B. Man in No.3

March

1 Monday

Shops: Farty Cushion
False Dung
Funny hat
Celery

Those two men in that house 8.30 ITV

AVOID

IN

2 Tuesday

winding down

March

3 Wednesday

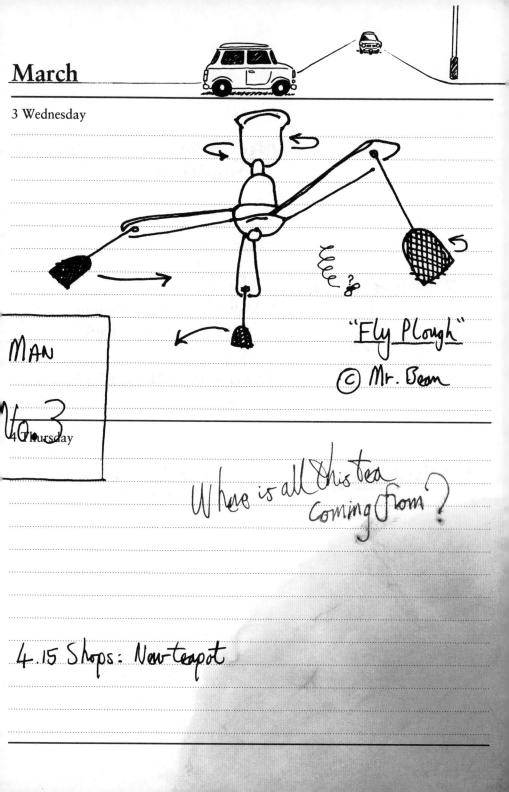

"Fly Plough"

© Mr. Bean

MAN

to 3

4 Thursday

Where is all this tea coming from?

4.15 Shops: New teapot

March

5 Friday

9.00　N.B. Order Flowers for Grandad　✓　⟵

2.00　Ring Grandma　AAARGH!

RING FLORIST
RING FLORIST

Funny Man with wart 10.00 ITV

6 Saturday

9.00　RING FLORIST

7 Sunday

9.00　RING FLORIST

March

8 Monday

⟶ GRANDAD is 90ᵗʰ BIRTHDAY (Quite AMAZING REALLY)

RING FLORIST : CHANGE MESSAGE

3pm Grandad Funeral

9 Tuesday

Send off for Shirley Bassey Mug (Large)
to: Shirley's Mug (Large)
P.O. Box 203
Swindon
Wilts. SN43 7PZ

"PORTABLE PHONE"

© Mr. Bean

March

10 Wednesday

3.00pm Ring Irma Gobb — leave funny noises
on Answering Machine
(sobbing?)

11 Thursday

PINK TICKET NO. 77

KEEP IT SAFE

Draw: 27 March

GRAND RAFFLE

In Aid of Police
Benevolent Fund

1st Prize:
A Week
in the Bahamas

2nd Prize:
Dinner for Two at Pizza Hut

12 Friday

THE FLOWER

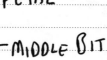

PETAL

MIDDLE BIT

7.30 Botany Club

---

13 Saturday   **14 Sunday**

LEAF   OTHER LEAF

GROUND

LITTLE ROOTS

ROOTS

WORM

March

15 ...nday

GOOD OMEN OR WHAT?

12 DAYS TILL

16 Tuesday

RAFFLE

8.15 Rajpoot Tandoori
(Table for One)

March

17 Wednesday   St Patrick's Day

Shops: Loo paper (x6)

TEN DAYS

MURPHY'S

PALE STREET

LUKE'S PASSAGE

Avoid Murphy's Bar

18 Thursday

NINE DAYS

FRAZZLE
FRAZZLE

JACKET

BAHAMAS

"RAFFLE PRIZE"

©Mr. Bean   (no copycats)

March

19 Friday

EIGHT DAYS

10.30 Building Society
Take all money out
Put no money in

Holiday shopping: Shirts
Socks
Biscuits
Vaseline

Marmalade?

20 Saturday

SEVEN DAYS

Buy holiday shoes

21 Sunday

SIX DAYS

NO shops open
NO shopping
(except Vaseline)

OATH OATH OATH!

Corydalis Lutea

March

22 Monday

23 Tues

FIVE DAYS

4.15 Buy holiday shirts

FOUR DAYS

2 — 4.45
Holiday shopping spree spree spree spr

March

24 Wednesday

Buy holiday socks ✓

25 Thursday

Ring Building Soc
— no money

Buy holiday celery ✓

If ⌂ + @ + !!! + ℳ = ✸

and ⊓ + ❀ — ▣ = △

What is ▣ ?

MAD MAD
MAD MAD

(4 APRIL)

March

26 Friday

1

FINAL CHECKLIST: MOSQUITO STUFF
FILM
CROCODILE KNIFE
SNAKE GREASE
SPOON

Buy holiday underpants
(both types)

ooh!

27 Saturday

10.55 Cross Fingers

11.00 RAFFLE
DRAW
St. Andrew's Church
Hall

BLAST
OFF

28 Sunday

Travel to
Barbados
on plane

March

29 Monday

Raffle Mystery

THE RAFFLE held in aid of the Police Benevolent Fund was shrouded in mystery last night after the winning ticket number 77 could not be found. The draw had to be held

Arrive in Barbados

Where the blasted heck is that raffle ticket?

30 Tuesday

KILL! SLAY! DAMCUSS!

Barbados

11.00 Start drinking beer

Aster Alpinus

31 Wednesday

Drink beer all day

Barbados

POL-ICE
Station
Help

Samaritans
2367925

and all night

1 Thursday   April Fool's Day

Barbados

11.45
N°3.

Dear Mr Bean,
A parcel arrived
for you while you
were out. I have
it with me.

Man in N°3.
(down hall).

11.15 Man out –
try later

2.10 No Man

4.42 No Man

April

2 Friday

~~Barbados~~

Where oh WHERE is Shirley Bassey mug ?

Ring Swindon

D. Plumb
Private Investigator
799

Try man in No. 3

~~7.50 Botany Club~~
Too depressed

3 Saturday

~~Barbados~~

~~Send back~~ Cliff Richard
mug. GET OUT CLIFF
COME IN Shirley
WHERE ARE YOU??

4 Sunday

~~Barbados~~

$$\boxed{O} = \boxed{} + \check{O}$$

Try man
in No. 3

April

5 Monday

Barbados

Dear Mr. Plumb

I am distraught beyond measure. I have lost a raffle ticket No. 77 and I don't know where to put myself or what to do. I have lost all sense of direction and have forgotten how to make tea, even with a tea bag which is so simple really, isn't it? I last saw the ticket in my hand on March 17th. I don't know where it is. I'm sure I put it somewhere but now somebody called Caroline has gone to Barbados

6 Tuesday

Barbados

HATE
HATE HATE HATE

CAROLINE

Snakes → SSSSS

SSSSS

Ring Samaritans 236 7925 re. Raffle Crisis

NO ESCAPE

PLAN VIEW

April

7 Wednesday

8.30 Banana

8.30 No. 3.

Dear Mr Bean,
I know you have been
knocking on my door,
but I have been ignoring
you because there _is_
no parcel!

APRIL FOOL!!

Man in No. 3
(down hall).

8 Thursday

6.00 No Man

April

9 Friday   Good Friday

6.15 Steal Milk (No.3)

~~Barbados~~

Send back Des O'Connor mug.

SEEDS: ~~Pansies~~ NO   Nasturtium ×
Deadly Nightshade ✓
Widow's Misery ✓   Love Lies Bleeding ✓

(7.30 Botany Club)

10 Saturday

~~Barbados~~

10.10 Goringe's (seeds)

11.00 Plant seeds

8.10 All About Terrapins
(David Attenborough Borough)
BBC 2

11 Sunday   Easter Day

Boiled Egg

Seeds growing

April

12 Monday   Easter Monday

Terrapin Budget:

Glass tank	£ 69 — 95		Seeds Growing
Water	£ 0 — 00		
Filter	£ 15 — 95		
Heater	£ 25 — 50		
Gravel	£ 8 — 00	from shop	
	£ 0 — 00	from next door's drive	
Weed	£ 2 — 50	from shop	
	£ 0 — 00	from next door's garden	
Terrapin	£ 0 — 20p	↑ CHEAP	

13 Tuesday

I love
Mr. Bean

Seeds Growing

Terry the
Terrapin

April

14 Wednesday

Shirley Bassey mug
arrives HOORAY!

Seeds growing

11.00 Lovely hot steaming mug* of Tea mmmmmmmmmmmmmmm!

15 Thursday

Seeds still growing

10.15 Pet Shop — Buy Terrapin

3pm Christening (of Terry)

* Shirley Bassey type, large

April

16 Friday

Seeds growing?

This makes me so cross

17 Saturday

10.00 Check Seeds

Oh, bosoms

18 Sunday

Seeds RUINED
(DOG)

April

19 Monday

9.15 Buy seeds
9.45 Sow seeds

New seeds: Monkey Flower ✓   Red hot poker ✓
             Baby's breath (UURGH)   Stinking Helibore ✓

             ~~Devil-in-a-bush~~ stupid

                                    Plant seeds

20 Tuesday

5.45 am Creep out and steal milk

                                    Seeds growing

                              ← RUDDY MOUSE
                                   PRINTS

Ring Samaritans

(Keep them talking)

April

21 Wednesday   Queen's Birthday   Ring?

(New) Seeds should still be growing

"MOUSETRAP MR.1"

© Mr. Bean

22 Thursday   5.50am Ssssssssshhhhhh Steal more milk

Wossit
  Grossit
Twissit
    Fossit

Seeds growing

That really funny one 7.00 Ch.4

April

23 Friday

SNAP !

10.00 Check seeds
To sum up: 1. Nothing happening
2. No little green bits.
3. No flowers.
4. No nothing.
5. No good.

CUSS CUSS
CUSS CUSS
CUSS

SEED MAN —

25,000,000,000
000,000,000,000
000,000 000,000,
000,000 000,000,
TONS

24 Saturday

N° 3.

Dear Mr Bean,
Milk bottles are
frequently stolen
from outside my
door. Can you
throw any light
on the matter.
Man in N° 3
(down hall).

25 Sunday

He must be really stupid

April

26 Monday

YabadabadabadabadabadabadabadabadabadabadabadabadabadabadOOOO!

——>·

27 Tuesday

That grizzly man who was in that old Police programme with
Inspector Morse and ran off with the leggy dancer
8.30 BBC1

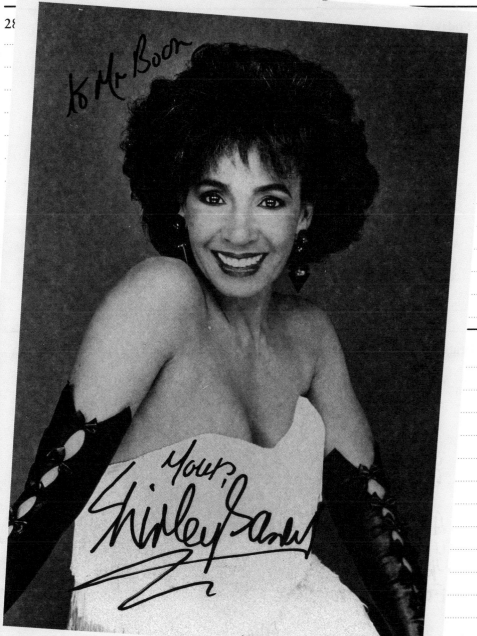

April/May

30 Friday

If you make a jelly in a teapot
And try to flop it out
It takes about a fortnight
To get it out the spout

1 Saturday

Mayday mayday
All around
Ship in fog
Big hooting sound

All that noise and fuss
you make
keep it down
For goodness sake!

2 Sunday

Write to Shirley
Bassey re. her
lovely mug

(v. v. v. v. v. v. v.
v. v. v. important)

3 Monday May Day

"FOOT REST"
© Mr. Bean

---

4 Tuesday

2-3 Give us an S	S	
Give us a T	T	
Give us a u	U	
Give us a p	P	
Give us an i	I	
Give us a d	D	
Give us an m	M	
Give us an a	A	
Give us an n	N	
Give us an i	I	
Give us an n	N	
Give us an n	N	

Give us an o   O
Give us a .   ٠
Give us a 3   3

What is that spell?

STUPIO MAN

IN No. 3

kill kill kill

Yes Yes Yes

May

Highbury District Council
Council Offices
Highbury, London N10

Mr Bean,
c/o Mrs Wickets,
Daffodils.
Room 2, 12 Arbor Road,
London N10

15th May 1993

Dear Mr Bean

Thank you very much for your letter of the 5th May concerning, as you see it, the "outrageous" shape of your toilet.

Unfortunately, the obligations of your local council extend only as far as the provision of sewage facilities in the borough, and we cannot be held responsible for the shape of any individual apparatus. Certainly the shape of the pan you describe (your drawings are returned herewith) would appear to be traditional.

I was naturally distressed to hear of the effect that this "mad toilet" is having on your mental health. Your nightmares, accompanied, as you claim, by the "banshee howls" akin to the sound of "two enmeshed chainsaws (two-stroke)" would only become the responsibility of the local authority if complaints were received from other tenants at Daffodils. This department has no record of any such correspondence.

I therefore cannot entertain your request for a Community Charge rebate, merely on the basis of the "horrifying scenes" you describe, and the blame which you directly attribute to the curvature of your lavatory.

Yours sincerely

G.M. Nuttall

May

7 Friday

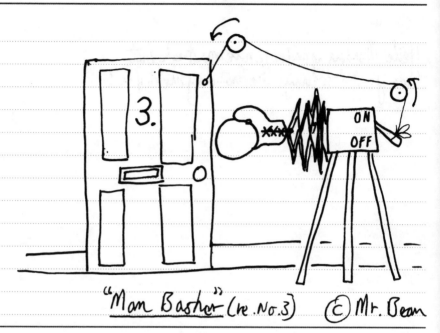

3.

"Man Basher" (re. No.3)   © Mr. Bean

8 Saturday

TEE HEE HEE

9 Sunday

9.15 Rubbish

10.00 More Rubbish

May

← CHICKEN SOUP.

10 Monday

Hello Monday you look nice and fresh, but
then you're always the first day aren't you?

11 Tuesday

Oh Tuesday goodness me
you've come along too, how delightful.
How do you do?

May

12 Wednesday

of a fright there Wednesday although OOOpp! Gave me a bit expected you, I know, because you always bowl up on Day 3.

Sit down, do.

I've got some bitter lemon if you'd like some but nothing alcoholic I'm afraid (Burp)

Oh, and Wednesday this is Thursday.

13 Thursday

Oh, you've met, I'm sorry. You met last week?

How interesting!

Silly me.

May

14 Friday

FRIDAY where have you **been**?

I've been so anxious. You're always so late, you naughty boy, the week's nearly over. Honestly.

---

15 Saturday

Brr Brr. Brr Brr.
Ting.

Hello? Yes Mr. Beanhere. Can you not make it Saturday? But it's the sixth day, and you're expected. Oh tish pish posh.

16 Sunday

The Lord's Day

(not my responsibility)

May

17 Monday

THE GROCER (Caught Unawares)

~~Blancmange~~
~~Stonehenge~~
Nothing rhymes with Orange
Except perhaps Lozenge.

18 Tuesday

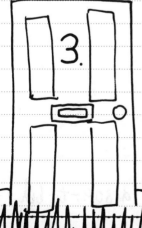

3.

© Mr. Bean

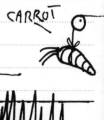

CARROT

May

19 Wednesday   8.15 Get up.

Ring Irma Gobb

Join Poetry Class 7.30
(Ms. Rosemary
Haseburg)

10.30 Go to bed

20 Thursday   8.15 Get up

If I had a rant   Poetry research: Buy daffodils
I'd have a pursuit.   Ring T.S. Eliot

9.30 Go to bed

21 Friday

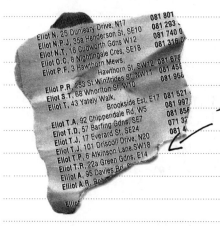

Eliot N, 25 Dunleary Drive, N17   081 801
Eliot N.P.J, 35a Henderson St, SE10   081 293
Eliot N.T, 16 Cudworth Gdns W12   081 740 0
Eliot O.C, 8 Nightingale Cres, SE18   081 316 0
Eliot P.F, 3 Hawthorn Mews,
     Hawthorn St, SW12   081 679
Eliot P.R, 253 St Winifrides St, NW11   081 456
Eliot S.T, 68 Whorlton St, W10   081 956
Eliot T, 43 Yately Walk,
     Brookside Est, E17   081 521
Eliot T.A, 92 Chippendale Rd, W5   081 997
Eliot T.D, 57 Barfing Gdns, SE7   081 856
Eliot T.J, 17 Everard St, SE24   071 37
Eliot T.P, 6 Atkinson Lane, SW18   081 4
Eliot T.R, 22a Green Gdns, E14
Eliot A, 95 Davies Rd
Eliot A.R.
Eliot

T.S. Eliot ex-directory?

10.30 Go to bed (Boring)

---

22 Saturday

9.30 Get up (Yippee!)

23 Sunday

Don't get up

If I haven't got up then I won't have to go to bed
HOORAY!

10.30 Go to bed.

May

24 Monday

Ring Irma Gobb
And keep it clean
If you get
Answer machine.

Shirley Bassey in Pro-Am Golf   8.00 BBC2

25 Tuesday

DAM DAM DAM DAM DAM
DAM DAM DAM DAM DAM
DAM DAM DAM
DAM

26 Wednesday

Poem: <u>ATTENTION MICE</u>

You'd better watch out
Cos if I see you about
You're going to end up in my mincer
Then no mucking about
I'll scrape you all out
And do the same thing to your sister

7.30 Poetry Class

27 Thursday

"<u>MOUSETRAP MK. 2</u>"

© Mr. Bean

May

28 Friday

9.00 Buy Fish

Leave out all day

29 Saturday

Leave out all day

30 Sunday

← Really smelly now.

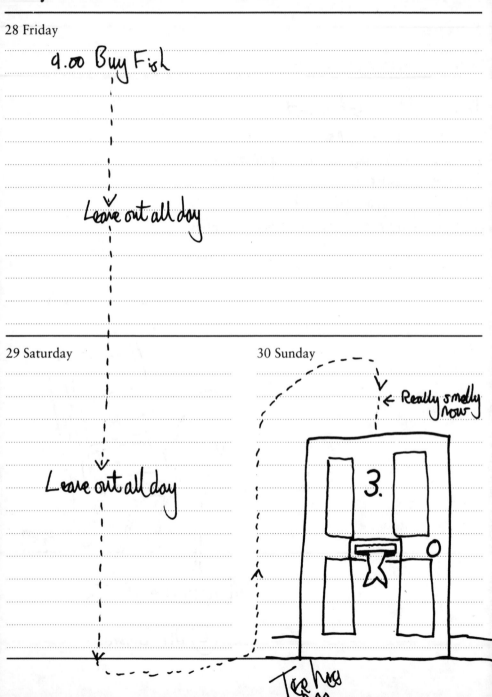

3.

Tee hee hee

May/June

c3.

31 Monday

Up at nine
Out by ten
Drive to town
Drive home again

Those two men in that house 8.00 ITV

1 Tuesday

HOUSEFLY

FILTH

"HOUSE FLY TRAP"

© Mr Bean

June

2 Wednesday

Picnic shopping : Tea Bag
Lettuce
Sticklebacks in Brine

1.00 Picnic in Park.

Cilla Black
Has a lack
(but) Shirley Witley
Is a cuddly girley

7.30 Poetry Class   (Bassey)

3 Thursday

Don't do ANYTHING today AT ALL

except go to the toilet

June

C3.

---

4 Friday

Oh Lord who giveth and taketh away, taketh away Terry and put him in a nice big tank in heaven and remember to feed him because I forgot

Amen.

Terry (the Terrapin) R.I.P.

---

5 Saturday

Give Terry's tank, water, weeds, and gravel away to somebody ——
↳ Oxfam?

HELP FEED STARVING TERRAPINS ALL OVER THE WORLD

6 Sunday

Help on it's way

OFF

June

7 Monday

There's a poetry test
I'm sure to pass
In Ms Rosemary Rosebury's
Poetry Class
She's given us the title
"A Goddess Sublime"
Which will take no time
For the Prince of Rhyme (to do)

8 Tuesday

9.45 Turn in

POETIC LICENCE
ALL
CATEGORIES
EXPIRES: 7 JUNE 1994
MR BEAN   MALE

3.

A GODDESS SUBLIME

by Mr. Bean

If there's anything in the world
That I would like to be
It's Shirley Bassey's microphone
So she could sing to me

I know she sings to everyone
When they come to hear her
But front row seats cost fifteen quid
And I would be much nearer.

Another thing that strikes me

7.30 Poetry Class

About being up that close

Is that I could smell her perfume
And see right up her nose*

I know microphones get dribbled on
But so what, what the hell?
It is a perk of the job when it's Shirley's gob
And I'd get in free as well!

* N.B. Check with Ms. Hasebury — close & nose rhyme

June

Poo-ee!

Ring Samaritans
re. drains

12 Saturday

13 Sunday

11.15 Forget it

Get up early tomorrow

June

14 Monday

11.10 Give blood

15 Tuesday

~~Dear Council~~
~~Nurse Gibley~~,

Wash out
Jam Jar

Dear Blood Man/Woman

I would like to become a blood donor and enclose, for your perusal,

June

16 Wednesday

Highbury Royal Infirmary
Highbury, London N10

re: 16 June
from: Highbury Royal Infirmary

Dear Mr Bean

Although we are pleased that you have decided to become a blood donor, I'm afraid that we cannot accept donations by post. We have disposed of your blood in accordance with the conditions of the Medicines Act 1709, and your jam jar is returned herewith.

Perhaps you would like to give blood when a mobile unit visits your area? If you would like further information, please see your doctor.

17 Thursday

Perhaps you will be seeing your doctor anyway?

Yours sincerely

Jose Manteras

Jose Manteras
Doctor

June

CRASH!

18 Friday

"GRISTLE MASTER"

© Mr. Bean

19 Saturday

Shops: Loaf
Butter
Egg (x2)
Spindle
Grommet

20 Sunday

June

21 Monday

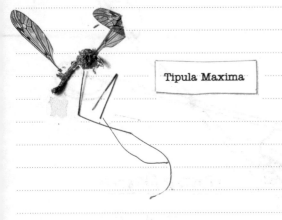

Tipula Maxima

6.00 Lance Boil

22 Tuesday

9.15 Lance Boil

6.15 Ring Lance Boil

7.45 Entymology Club
↳ What is Entymology?

June

23 Wednesday

Morning: Go to Library

...tas -utis f. _integer_: see ENTIRE]
...e /ɪnˈtaɪt(ə)l/ _v.tr._ **1 a** (usu. foll. by _to_) give (a
person etc.) a just claim. **b** (foll. by _to_ + infin.) give
(a person etc.) a right. **2 a** give (a book etc.) the title
of. **b** _archaic_ give (a person) the title of (_entitled him
sultan_). □□ **entitlement** _n._ [ME f. AF _entitler_, OF
entiteler f. LL _intitulare_ (as IN-², TITLE)]
entity /ˈentɪtɪ/ _n._ (_pl._ -**ies**) **1** a thing with distinct
existence, as opposed to a quality or relation. **2** a
thing's existence regarded distinctly. □□ **entitative**
/-tətɪv/ _adj._ [F _entité_ or med.L _entitas_ f. LL _ens_ being]
ento- /ˈentəʊ/ _comb. form_ within. [Gk _entos_ within]
entomb /ɪnˈtuːm/ _v.tr._ **1** place in or as in a tomb. **2**
serve as a tomb for. □□ **entombment** _n._ [OF _entomber_
(as EN-¹, TOMB)]
entomo- /ˈentəməʊ/ _comb. form_ insect. [Gk _entomos_
cut up (in neut. = INSECT) f. EN-² + _temnō_ cut]
entomology /ˌentəˈmɒlədʒɪ/ _n._ the study of the
forms and behaviour of insects. □□ **entomological**
/-məˈlɒdʒɪk(ə)l/ _adj._ **entomologist** _n._ [F _entomologie_
or mod.L _entomologia_ (as ENTOMO-, -LOGY)]

← BINGO!

24 Thursday

TEE HEE HEE
HEE HEE

ANGRY IRMA

June

25 Friday

11.00 MFI (Cupboard - self assembly)

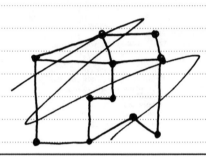

26 Saturday

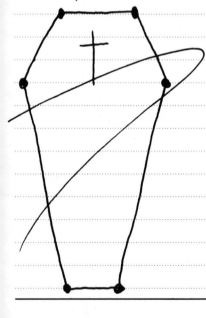

27 Sunday

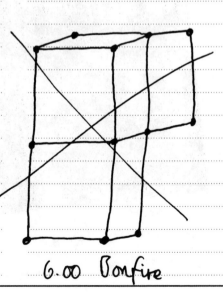

6.00 Bonfire

June

28 Monday

Oh what a horrible morning oh what a horrible day
I've got a horrible feeling that people Just get in my way

but only ONCE

and then it's CURTAINS

29 Tuesday

for them

Hehhyhhahahhteh
heh hhhhh

Yesterday up on the stairs
I caught a man unawares

I gave him a fright again today
By taking both his ears away

7.45 Entymology Club
(Spelling 10/10)

(You should have seen him

June/July

30 Wednesday

6.00 News (BBC) De de doom de de doomm de de dun dum dum dum doo doo doo dum dum doo doo dum downnnnn... ...This is the Six O'Clock News from the BBC with thingummy jig and whats her face...... de de doom de de drum.

1 Thursday

Tenebrio Molitor

10.00 News at Ten (ITV)
(Pay attention)

2 Friday

Shops: Shake 'n Vac

12.00 Clean Jacket (Tweed)

---

3 Saturday

9.20 Go out
10.04 Come in
10.24 Go out again
12.10 Come in again
1.45 Go out again
2.05 Come in again
2.55 Go out again.
2.56 Come in again
2.57 Go out again
4.50 Come in again
6.03 Go out again
6.43 Forget to come in again
7.00 Miss Programme
7.28 Eventually come in again

4 Sunday

CANCELLED

July

5 Monday

Ring Irma Gobb?

No, can't be bothered.

I would very much like to go to the moon, even though I don't like travel, as a rule. No language problems, and no crowding.

6 Tuesday Also, no air. GASP GASP GASP

9.10 Over the moon about something

7.45 Entymology Club lots of creepy crawlies

July

7 Wednesday

Young people with ~~funny~~ horrible accents 5.40 BBC1

8 Thursday

Shopping (to service car):
GREASE
OIL
EGG WHISK
& Filter
Coffee
G Funibles
Spotting spigot

Fairy Liquid
Alarm clock?
Bottle (don't lose it)

July CAR SERVICING

(PHOTO GUIDE)

9 Friday

STUFF REQUIRED

ENGINE
(LOCATION OF)

10 Saturday

CHANGE FILTER

TOP UP RADIATOR

CHANGING THE OIL

TOUCH-UP PAINTWORK

BEFORE

AFTER

CHANGE BULB IN BOOT

ALL DONE!

Entymology Club 7.45

July

14 Wednesday

OLD Getting dressed procedure: First   Shirt
                                  then   Socks
                                  then   Underpants
                                  then   Trousers
                                  then   Shoes
                                  then   Tie
                                  then   Belt
                          BORING then   Jacket

15 Thursday

NEW Getting dressed procedure:

First Shirt   First Shoes   First Trousers
then Jacket   then Socks   then Undies
then Tie   Stupid   Stupid then Impossible
                                                  Stupid
                                                  Barmy

    First Belt   First
    then Tie   then   Undies
    then Shoes   then   Jacket
    then Leave House   Mad mad
         Too rude   Mad

then Jail

July

16 Friday

10.45 Library   Return   "Gone with the Wind"
                            "Stand and Deliver"

                 Get out   "Insects of Yesteryear" by E. Dalton

                    "The Land of Gore" by Zak Brood
                    "Limb from Limb" by Zak Brood
                          (Parts 1 & 2)

                    "Are you bleeding comfortably?"
                             (Z. Brood)

<u>also Ask Gobb to Pictures</u>

17 Saturday

8.10 HORROR FILM

18 Sunday

10.15 Vicar (Exorcism)

Sleep with light on

July

19 Monday

Seek Professional Help.

North London
Technical College
Highbury, London N10

Mr Bean,   16th July 1993
c/o Mrs Wickets,
Daffodils,
Room 2, 12 Arbor Road,
London N10

Dear Mr Bean

I'm sure that I need not reiterate the horror and revulsion felt by all of us when you revealed your pressed insect collection. It is inhuman to murder God's creatures in this way, merely to form a macabre collection in the pages of your diary.

There has been a unanimous decision taken by our sub-committee to report your behaviour to the RSPCA, from whom I hope you will be hearing soon.

You really are a quite revolting man.

Dr Legge

Dr. Legge
Sec., Entomology Club

20 Tuesday

CRASH!

July

21 Wednesday

Seek Professional Help re. Nightmares

Can't sleep

GGAAAAGH

22 Thursday

Can't sleep

Clossiana Euphrosyne

July

23 Friday

Smiths Do-It-All : 1 Mirror
: 1 Wooden stake

Sainsburys : 10 lbs Garlic

Sleep with light on

24 Saturday

25 Sunday

8.30 Holy Communion
9.30 Family Service
11am Mattins

Lock door
Sleep with light on

6.30 Evensong
(Attend religiously)

July

Stay in all day

Breathe quietly

idea: The Exorcist

SSSSSS SSSSSsss hhhhhhhhhh ---

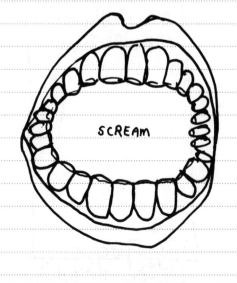

SCREAM

Pull myself
together.

July

28 Wednesday

Close my eyes
Up tight and sing

Go away
You big bad thing!
Open them again
And shout   GO AWAY

GE

29 Thursday

NEW
SECURITY
ARRANGEMENTS

July/August

30 Friday

6.00 Shirley Bassey
Master Chefs

or you'll

31 Saturday

1 Sunday

A CLOUT!

CRASH

August

2 Monday

Feeling much better today, thank you.

Shops: Beans
Bread

Long Johns

3 Tuesday

9.45 Mrs. Wicket (Root)

7.15 Burn something
(Mrs. Wicket?)

August

4 Wednesday

Significant disturbances.

Beans for dinner
Beans for tea
Oh windy Bean
Oh windy me

5 Thursday

Further disturbances (Bottom Dept.)

HONEY

© Mr. Bean

August

6 Friday 8.30 Take Mini to Mum

A. & G. MOTORS
10 Ugly Street, Twickenham
081 851 1590

7 Satur

Dear Mr Bean

Thought you should know, that your mini is
a Dog. We looked at it this morning. and it
is completely clapped. You need a new sub
frame mate and by ends and mounts and
exhaust etc to name but a few. Tires
are as bald as that swimmer bloke. We're
talking a lot of <u>cash</u>. like two or three
hundred also the brown stuffs everywhere
(you been driving fast again!!!!!!!) No I
mean the rust its terrible the car is
really shot. My feet went through the
floor at Sainsburys roundabout, Fred
Flintstone Eat your heart out!!! Come to
the garage and you better say what you
want cos we're going to Rimini Tuesday

Graham

P.S. My mate thinks you're weird

9 Monday

"HANDY ASH"

© Mr. Bean

10 Tuesday

12.00 Park

Dear ~~Highbury Us~~ Council Man

The state of the park is very outrageous and, in a way, catadysmic, it is so smelly. I know I may have contributed to the aroma myself recently, because as you may know, I have had my own problems, but the poop is the matter that

August

11 Wednesday

12 Thursday

"Daffodils"
12 Arbor Rd.
LONDON N10

BEAN ANTI-POOP ASSOCIATION (BAPA)

Dear Resident,
I hope you are well. I am fine. I am writing to ask if, like me, you are sick and tired of too much poop. Dogs, treat this road, and the park, like a huge toilet, which it isn't. Join BAPA and help me stamp out poop. Any dog owner caught ~~fouling our paths~~ allowing a dog to foul our paths will get a right dressing down, and further abuse. Those responsible for more than one poop will get a punch up the bracket. (We could take it in turns)

If you are interested, please fill in this form, and send it back.

— — — — — — — ✂ — — — — — — — — —

NAME . . . .
ADDRESS . . . .

- -

I think your idea is great. Signed.

- -

13 Friday

9.45 Library (Photocopies). n/f. Too much poop (BAPA)

Ring Samaritans
re. poop.

14 Saturday

15 Sunday

Do I like Golf?

IN →

August

16 Monday

ER.

B.A.P.A.   B.A.P.A.

DIEU ET MON DROIT

By Appointment To
Her Majesty The Queen
Poop Preventative And Dirt Disposal
Merchants Bean Anti-Poop Association

17 Tuesday

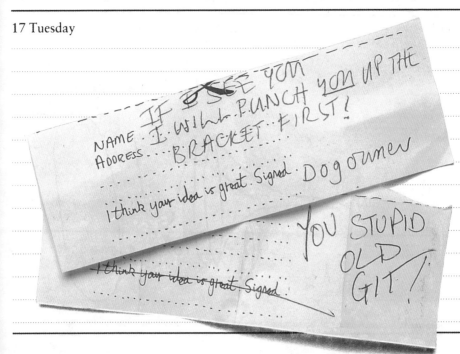

NAME IF I SEE YOU I WILL PUNCH YOU UP THE BRACKET FIRST!
ADDRESS

I think your idea is great. Signed DOG OWNER

I think your idea is great. Signed

YOU STUPID OLD GIT!

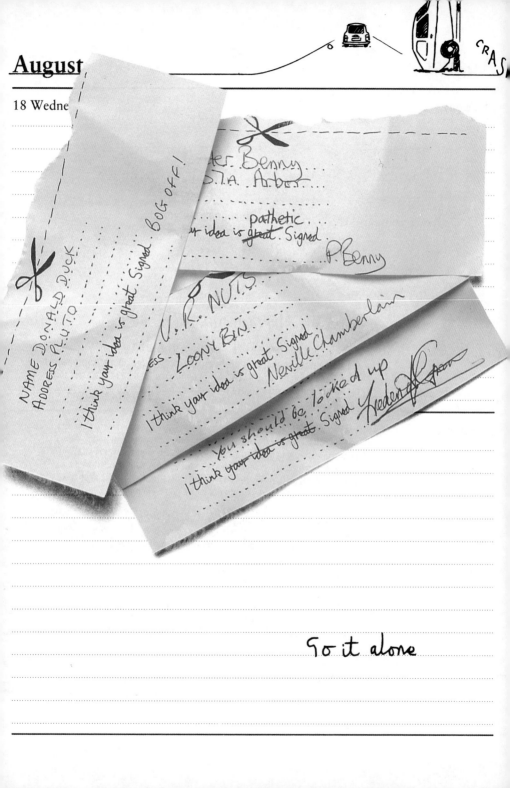

CRAS

...ter Benny...
...S.T.A. Arbor...
...r idea is ~~great~~. pathetic... Signed
P. Benny

NAME DONALD DUCK
ADDRESS PLUTO
I think your idea is great. Signed. BOG OFF!

...ess U.R. NUTS...
...LOONY BIN...
I think your idea is great. Signed
Neville Chamberlain

You should be locked up
I think your idea is great. Signed Frederic...

Go it alone

METROPOLITAN POLICE
4, Guildford Street
Highbury
London N10

Dear Mr. Bean

It has been drawn to our attention that you have been circulating letters to the residents in your area of the borough, complaining about the problem of dogs fouling the pavement. This is not a criminal offence in itself, but the blatant incitements to violence which are also contained therein most certainly are.

We received a complaint from a dog owner yesterday, claiming that he was recently attacked by a man answering to your description. After the complainant's pet had made an accidental deposit in the park, the attacker attempted to force the owner's nose into the excreta. This is not the kind of behaviour that upstanding citizens should have to suffer. The hooligan was also carrying a quantity of corks, with one of which he attempted to violate the dog.

If this attacker was yourself, you must appreciate that the Constabulary takes a very dim view of this kind of behaviour: if we hear of any similar incidents, or af any further letters, criminal proceedings will be brought against you.

Yours sincerely

Sgt. Rickers

Sgt. P.R.D. Rickers

August

23 Monday

9.00am Commence BAPA Stealth Deterrent Mk. 1

Glue	Tow bar
Soup	Pillow-case
Timber 24' x 1½" x 1½"	Electric Fan
Duvet Cover	Bed sheet
Broom handle	Screws
Bread Knife	Nails
	Horse Poop (½ Ton)

24 Tuesday

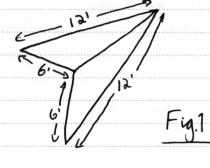

Fig.1

The fat man with the long hands 6.30 BBC1

August

25 Wednesday

Sore throat

I've got to be firmer
With Irma
If she's going to be
A long termer

Nose getting blogged

26 Thursday

Nose completely stuffed
Full of snot.   Chemist: Paraffin
                   Pipe cleaners?

4.00 Unfortunate snot accident (Mrs. Wicket)

August

27 Friday

Letter of Apology (Mrs. Wicket)

BAPA Deterrent: Fig 2

28 Saturday

Construction to continue apace.

9.00 Bonk bonk bonk

2.30 Tap tap tap tap

8.15 Kersplak Kersplak

29 Sunday

7.00 Bang bang bang bang
bang bang bink OWW!
Bang bang bang

August

30 Monday

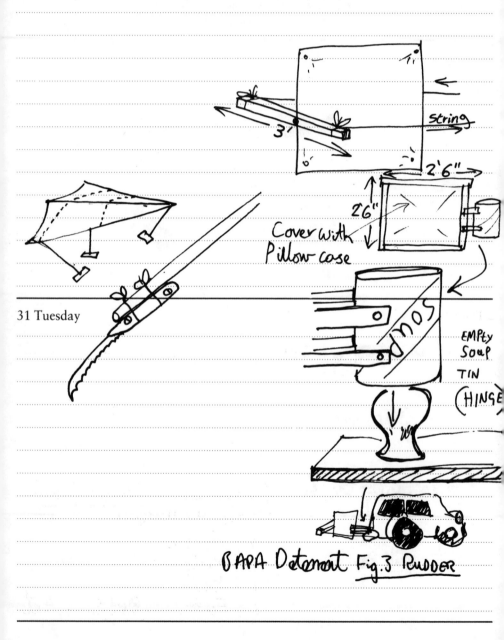

31 Tuesday

string

3'

2'6"

2'6"

Cover with
Pillow case

EMPTY
SOUP
TIN
(HINGE)

SOUP

BAPA Detonant Fig.3 RUDDER

September

1 Wednesday

MRS. WICKET IN BRIGHTON

10.00 Clear Drive
10.30 DELIVERY OF HORSE POOP

2 Thursday

Morning: Fill Duvet Cover with horse poop.

Recipe Idea: RABBIT STEW
2 pts. Hot Water
1   Rabbit
1   Plate
1   Knife
1   Fork   Boil, Serve, Eat.

September

3 Friday

Shops: More screws
        Bigger screws

N.B. Need to change Traffic Light sequence, Junction
of Arbor Road + New Road

Requirements: Screwdriver
              Pliers
              Mini
              Brain on
              Full Alert

4 Saturday   **5 Sunday**

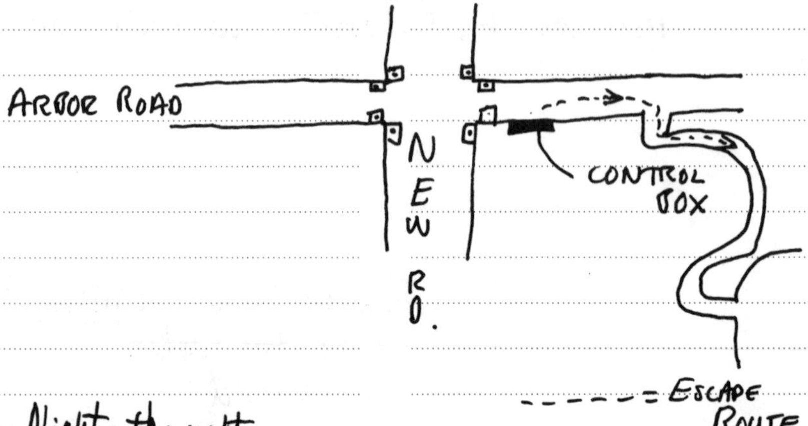

ARBOR ROAD

N
E
W

R
O.

CONTROL
BOX

- - - = ESCAPE
        ROUTE

Fig 4 Stealth Lights Plan

Saturday Nights the night
for fighting.
        (Stay in)

September

6 Monday

2 - 6pm Saw!
Saw!
Saw!

9'

BAPA Fig. 5

Lift
1,500 →
lbs

25 Forward
knots Speed

N
W — E
S

Looking Good
for Mon 13th.

September

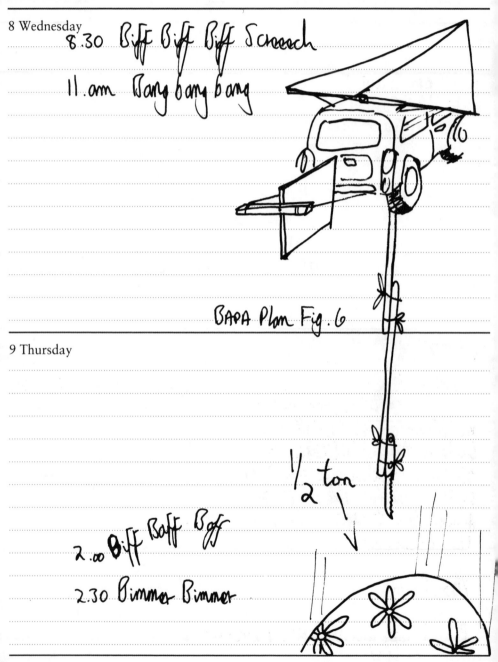

8 Wednesday

8.30 Biff Biff Biff Screech

11.am Bang bang bang

BAPA Plan Fig. 6

9 Thursday

½ ton

2.00 Biff Baff Boff

2.30 Bimmer Bimmer

10 Friday

N°3.

Mr Bean,
I have not slept
for three nights.
If the banging
does not stop I
will call the police.

Maria N°3.
(down hall.)

Oh, go away
and sit on a cabbage
(for the rest of your
life)

---

11 Saturday

Dear God
         Oh Lord, who giveth
and taketh away. Giveth me
luck on Monday but taketh me
not away; unless I do something
really lawful like forget to
flush the toilet
Yours sincerely

Mr. Bean

P.S. I hope you are well. I am fine.

12 Sunday

11.15 Church (Pray, pray,
                    pray)

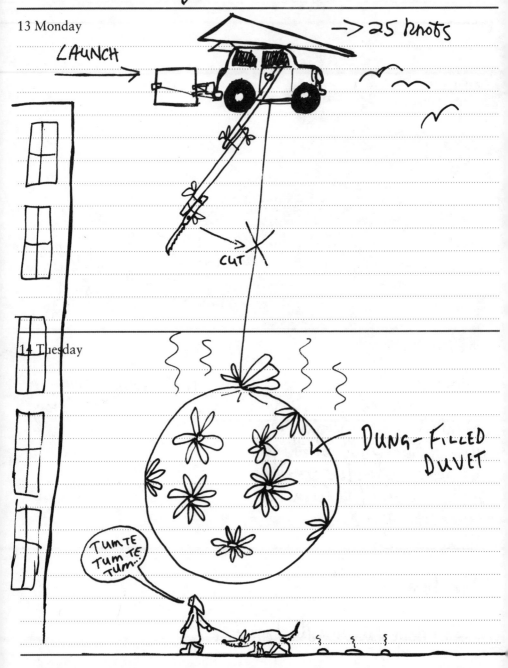

September

15 Wednesday

Highbury Herald September 15 1993

Bizarre man foiled

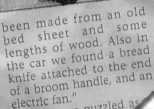

A HIGHBURY man's attempt to "put the world to rights" was foiled after police received a tip-off that a lime green mini was about to be launched from the roof of WH Smith in New Road.

The owner of the car, a Mr Bean of Arbor Road, Highbury, was first spotted by pedestrians on the street below, who alerted the police.

"The vehicle in question was fitted with a home-made set of wings, rather like a hang-glider, on the roof," said a police spokesman. "The wings upon inspection seem to have been made from an old bed sheet and some lengths of wood. Also in the car we found a bread knife attached to the end of a broom handle, and an electric fan."

Police are puzzled as Bean's possession of ton of hors...

Nagging thought (re. my origins)

4.45 Police Station

11.00 Further questioning.

September

17 Friday

Classifieds

METROPLOLITAN POLICE

DUNG
FOR SALE
(HORSE)
85p/5lb bag.
All proceeds to Police
Benevolent Fund
Reply box 77.

Large collection of inse
all in sil   sewoc
prese

Lie Low

18 Saturday

Lie Low

19 Sunday

Lie Lower

September

Dear Mr. Bean,
I don't believe your car was stolen at all. I saw the horse dung on the drive, and I think you are completely mad.

Man in Nº 3.
(down hall)

Nº 3.

I've a funny feeling my birthday was last Wednesday.

21 Tuesday

3.

STINK

© BEAN 1993

September

22 Wednesday

NAME Mr. D. Wilkinson
ADDRESS 23A Cherry Lane
London
N.5.
I think your idea is great. Signed.
D. Wilkinson

YIPPEE!!

23 Thursday

9.15 Ring Mr. Wilkinson

4.30 Mr. Wilkinson for tea

Shops: Crumpets   Stodgy cake
       Crusty buns   Lovely cake
       Juicy Cake   + other cake
       Big cake
       Small cake

September

24 Friday

NEW IMPROVED
"SNAIL" RULER

© Mr. Bean

J. 00 BANK - get £500
for Mr. Wilkinson

25 Saturday

10.00 Drive Mr. Wilkinson
to shops

J. 15 Mr. Wilkinson's ointment

26 Sunday

10.00 Polish Mr. Wilkinson's
knobs
+ knocker

Mr. Wilkinson borrowing
car this afternoon.

10.00 Car due back

September

27 Monday

WHERE IS MR. WILKINSON?

0AM STAB
CURSE WRETCH
DISM SMBER DISEMBOWEL

3.45 Police

WHERE OH WHERE IS MY LOVELY CAR

28 Tuesday

8.40 Catch bus to shops

9.20 Bus

4.30 Smelly bus home again

September

29 Wednesday

Poem: MIND YOUR GRANNY

If there's one thing that's not fetching
It is the sight of someone retching
So at Grandma's please do be extremely careful
If you need to vomit after tea
Then in the toilet you should be
So as not to give your Gran a sticky earful.

Mr. Bean 29 Sept 1993

7.30 Poetry Class

30 Thursday

Possible chorus: Pewky pewky retch retch
Head inside the bowl
Keeping it from Granny
Should be your intended goal.

Tra la

Show to Ms. Rosemary Hoseburn

October

1 Friday

WHERE is my £500?

WHERE is my car?

WHERE is slimy puss-y slimbag Mr. Wilkinson?

London Transport ⊖
PHOTOCARD

Name of holder

MR/M S

M. Bean

Valid for use only by person
shown with a ticket
bearing the same number.

T 5328

2 Saturday

I HATE THE BUSSSS

October

4 Monday

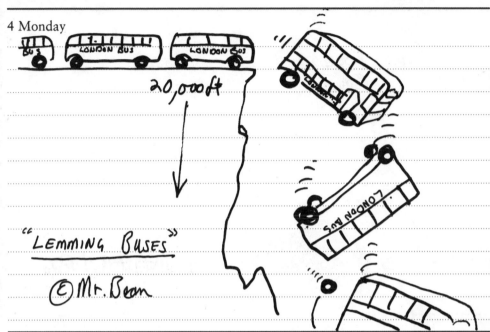

20,000 ft

" LEMMING BUSES "

© Mr. Bean

5 Tuesday

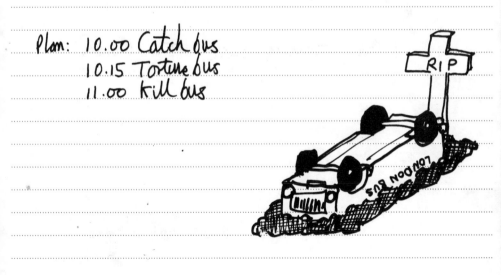

Plan: 10.00 Catch bus
10.15 Torture bus
11.00 Kill bus

RIP

October

6 Wednesday

Shops: Axe
Celery

7.00 Start Bell Ringing

7 Thursday

That revolting couple ITV (Morning)

9.30 Bell Ringing

October

8 Friday

1.45 am Bell Ringing

9 Saturday

11.00 More Bell ringing

Sunday

> Nº 3,
>
> Dear Mr Bean,
> Some idiot
> keeps ringing
> my doorbell
> then running
> away.
> Is it you?
>
> Man in Nº 3
> (down hall).

Hehyhehy
hehyheh
heh!

October

Highbury District Council (Adult Ed. Dept.)
Council Offices
Highbury, London N10

Dear Mr Bean

I am writing on what I know is a very sensitive subject, but I hope you will appreciate my honesty and frankness.

You have been a most enthusiastic pupil at my poetry class, never failing to do your homework and always handing in on time the work which I have requested. I am afraid that I have to tell you, however, that there is something about your work which is really quite shocking, not only to myself, but also to your classmates. They are forced to bear witness to your poetry, as you always insist on reading it out loud during the class, banging the lid of your desk enthusiastically as you do so. As I cannot emphasise enough, we have nothing but admiration for your enthusiasm. But we have had complaints. You may remember that Ann Warburton was physically sick during your stirring rendition of your poem on the same subject (Vomiting), and has never returned. Dear old Derek didn't sleep for a week after the blood-letting trilogy. The class is now half the size it was at the beginning of term, and I'm sorry to say that you and your poetry are the chief cause of the decline in numbers.

Might we interest you in another subject? The Adult Education Institute has over a hundred courses running in the '93-'94 academic year and I am sure we could find one more attuned to your inclinations and enthusiasm. Car maintenance? Italian? I'm sure we could find you something. If you choose to leave our poetry class, we would naturally refund your course fee in full, and also pay the new course's fees for a full five years.

Yours sincerely

Rosemary Hosebury

Rosemary Hosebury (Ms)

Yah boo hiss

I'm Mr. Dam Bean
Not Mr. Has Bean

As you might have guessed
You've made me depressed,

10.15. Buy bottle of alcohol in shop

October

13 Wednesday

I can do rhymes
Time after time (s)

Whiskey is lovely

French Foreign Legion
010 33 4 39 2 00 47

La Bla bla

TEA -CHERS

7·30 Poetry Class

14 Thursday

Shirley where are you
Shirley you understand

Ring Emma

More Gobble Wobble

Whisky

October

15 Friday

Do everything extremely quietly don't make any noise at all I think this might be what they call a hangover I've read about it in books move very slowly and speak very very softly do not go out close curtains sssssssssssshhhhh sssssssssshhh sss sssssshh

16 Saturday

9.30 Go out quietly
    Shopping: Bread
          Ear plugs

12.00 Come in so so quietly
      Tiptoe upstairs

ssssshh

17 Sunday

11.15 Don't go to church

18 Monday

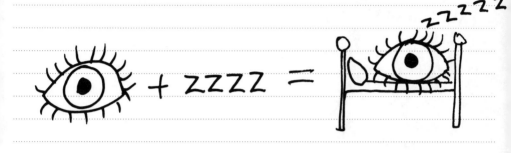

4.15 Lemon

19 Tuesday

6.40 CAR RETURNED YIPPEE!

God bless the Highland Police
Who returned my car
With its Raysse (still in it)

2.10 Put music system in car
(needs new stylus)

Records for car: The Very Best of Shirley Bassey
Shirley at her Best
Best of Bassey
Bassey's Best of the Bestest

October

---

20 Wednesday

MICK'S KENDO CLUB

School Hall, 8.15
Wednesday Evening

Shops: Broom Handles
White sheet

~~7.30 Poetry Class~~
8.15 Kendo Class

---

21 Thursday

Motor Show - Earl's Court

HOW TO GET THERE ON TIME

UWURRRMMM
URRRMM
URMMM

IGNORE
TRAFFIC
LIGHTS

---

22 Friday

110 MPH SAFE

SCREECH

BEEP BEEP

APPROACH PEDESTRIAN CROSSING:
1. HORN
2. ACCELERATE
3. CLOSE EYES

SQUEAL!

23 Saturday

24 Sunday

CHILDREN'S PLAYGROUND

HUMP BACKED BRIDGE

PEDESTRIAN PRECINCT

TRAFFIC JAM (TAKE SHORT CUT)

October

Petrol
Lettuce
Stamps

I thought girls
Always had curls

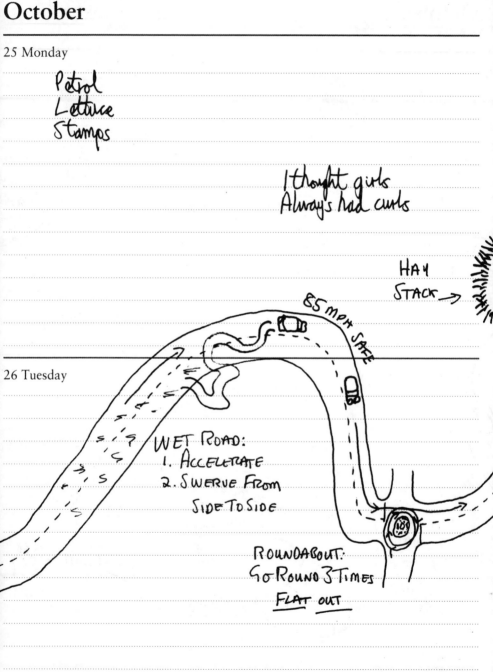

HAY
STACK →

85 mph SAFE

WET ROAD:
1. ACCELERATE
2. SWERVE FROM
   SIDE TO SIDE

ROUNDABOUT:
GO ROUND 3 TIMES
FLAT OUT

October

27 Wednesday

WARP SPEED

ROAD NARROWS

RELIANT ROBIN

POLICE CAR

NA NU NANU

OUT

8.15 Kendo Class

28 Thursday

Plan: 8.15 Go to Japan

12.30 Have lunch

Not possible

4.00 Come home

October

29 Friday

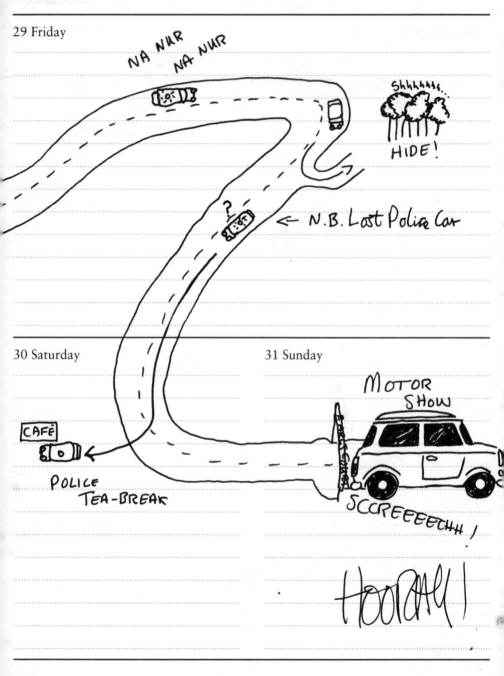

30 Saturday

31 Sunday

November

1 Monday

Oven broken — | ring Gas man |

Buy salad stuff : Tomatoes
Cucumber
Weeds
Insects
Soil

Dinner: Salad & Bread

2 Tuesday

9.00 Gas man

12.00 Oven still broken

stupid STUPID
Gas man

Lunch: Salad

Dinner: Salad

November

I HATE SALAD

Gas man

8.15: Try and cook without oven (Lamb chops)

9.00: FIRE BRIGADE

2.45am Sleep.

9.00 Shops: ~~Flour~~ Flour x 30 lbs
Eggs

Plot plot plot plot plot

November

Flipping dangerous (slippas!)

plot plot plot plot plot

Guy treason plot

treason treason plot

plot

Plot

8pm. Bonfire Party (in Park)

GET THEM WITH FLOUR BOMB

(then throw eggs)
if time

6 Saturday

9.00 Police Station
Questioning

all day

7 Sunday

Fireworks Fright

POLICE WERE CALLED to a bonfire party last night where a man was apprehended under suspicion of intending to plant a large explosive on the bonfire. "What we suspected of being a large bomb turned out to be a bag of flour and eggs", said event organiser Don Haze. "When I dragged him out of the tree he told me he was just about to make a cake."

Mr Bean, of Arbor Road, London, was detained at loca...

November

8 Monday

"COMMON SENSE"

© Mr. Bean

9 Tuesday

1.00 Egg

7.00 Another egg

METROPOLITAN POLICE
RECEIPT

your ref:

Surrendered Goods

our ref:

2 BROOM HANDLES

P.C.R.Leams

The above items have been confiscated pending
a decision by local magistrates

8.15
Mick's Kendo Club

Challenge Mick
to DUEL

5.15 Duel at Dawn

Requirements: Broom handle
Sheet

Report: 4.45 Hospital (re. neck brace)
6.00 Police (re. broom handles)

November

12 Friday

GOBB – GUMMER
The engagement is announced
between Irma Edith Gobb,
librarian, and Giles Gummer,
anaesthetist.

PACE – PARKES
The engagement is announced
between Carina Pace, video
producer, and Roger Parkes,
sculptor/cordon bleu ch

4.15 Stake out

WHAT!?!

13 Saturday

14 Sunday

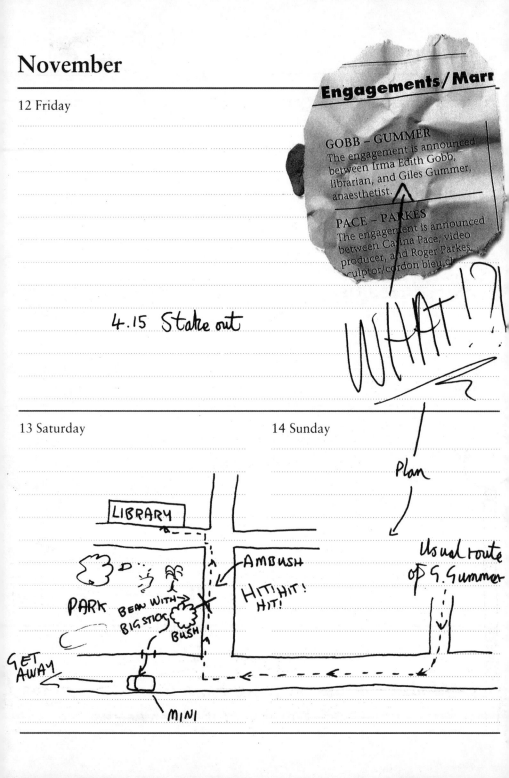

Plan

LIBRARY

AMBUSH

HIT! HIT!
HIT!

PARK

BEAN WITH
BIG STICK

BUSH

GET
AWAY

MINI

Usual route
of G. Gummer

15 Monday

SHIRLEY BASSEY LETTER

ʊ. ʊ. ʊ. ʊ. ʊ. ʊ. ʊ. ʊ. ʊ. ʊ. ʊ. ʊ. important

4.10 POST BOX

16 Tuesday

If I was going to choose a day
I would choose Choose-day.

4.07 Gummer Ambush POLICE SUSPICIOUS

HIDE DIARY

GUMMER 2

STRETCH

TUG

November

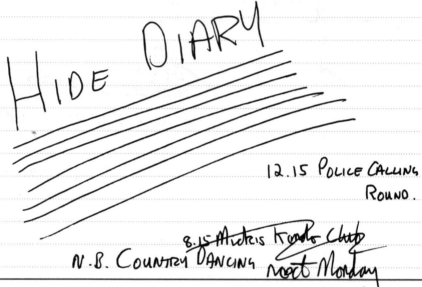

HIDE DIARY

12.15 POLICE CALLING
ROUND.

8.15 Audeis Treads Club
N.B. COUNTRY DANCING next Monday

TOAST RECIPE

Bum Bread
Eat

19 Friday

Shirley Bassey
Entertainments

Las Vegas • Hollywood • Monte Carlo • London

Mr Bean
c/o Mrs Wickets
"Daffodils"
Room 2
12 Arbor Road
London N10

Dear Mr Bean

Thank you for your recent letter to Ms Bassey: I'm sorry I've been so late in replying.

I am sorry to say that the vocal microphones used by Ms Bassey during her performances are extremely expensive items, and it would be impossible to send them as souvenirs to fans who request them.

Enclosed is a signed photograph as partial compensation!

Yours sincerely

Richard Kershaw

Richard Kershaw
Technical Manager
Shirley Bassey Ents.

Write again

November

22 Monday

START→

1 — 2 Tum TeeTum Tra la la

7.00 Country Dancing

23 Tuesday

Jump

AIRBORNE

TWIST

(Tum) Tra la-la -te tum tum tiddle tiddle

24 Wednesday

Boff   Boff

Dum   Bang   Trrrrummm   Titty

Bang

Deedee
Deedee
Dee

Vooop!

25 Thursday

Hop

Skip

La -la -la

teedly — dee   Bink   Bink   Boodle   Baff

FINISH

November

26 Friday

Shirley Bassey
Entertainments

Las Vegas • Hollywood • Monte Carlo • London

Mr Bean
c/o Mrs Wickets
"Daffodils"
Room 2
12 Arbor Road
London N10

Dear Mr Bean

I acknowledge receipt of your letter of the 17th of July.

27 Saturday

I understand that we misread the request in your last letter, and that there was no grammatical error. Your request was to BE one of Ms Bassey's microphones, rather than to posses one.

I should warn you that, in accordance with the policy of this office, your letter has been passed to the police.

Yours sincerely

Adrian Silverman
for Shirley Bassey Ents.

November

29 Monday <u>Mrs. Wicket going to Bournemouth</u>

Look after Kipper

KIPPER

Please look after
Kipper. He is
very sensitive and
needs feeding
every day
Mrs Wicket

7.00
Country Dancing
Tra-la-la-dee-dum-te-tum

1-2 1-2 1-2 1-2 and rest.

25 days to Christmas

December

N° 3.

Dear Mr Bean,
Have you heard
that barking from
Mrs Wicket's?

Man in N° 3.
(down hall).

It is you that's
barking!
Nagging thought

2 Thursday

Nagging thought

December

3 Friday

Nagging thought

4 Saturday

8.00 Nagging tho

oh my God NO
AAAARGHH

12 MIDNIGHT: Put Kipper's
corpse in middle of road
(Act natural)

5 Sunday

MRS. WICKET BACK
FROM BOURNEMOUTH

Dear Mrs. Wicket
I was so sorry to hear that
Kipper had escaped and been run
over while my back was turned.
I think I was ironing at the time,
although I did hear brakes
and, thinking it was a bat screeching
sub-sonically,

December

6 Monday

11am Funeral (Kipper)

THINKS →

1.15 Sink blocked

7 Tuesday

Ring Madame Sandra

2.00 Madame Sandra

No luck

December

8 Wednesday

11.00 Madame Sandra
(Some progress)

Mum's
ghost?

Madame Sandra

9 Thursday

11.45 Madame Sandra

MADE CONTACT WITH Mum

Question: Where is the plunger for the sink?
Answer: Under the stairs

12.10 Unblock sink ✓

ALL IN ONE STUMPS
© Mr. Bean

December

10 Friday

1.00 Crisps

11 Saturday

2 weeks till

Chrizzy

12 Sunday

December

13 Monday

9.15 Madame Sandra
(Talk to Charles Dickens)

Q: What was supposed to
happen to Edwin Drood?

A: Hadn't made up his mind.

14 Tuesday

Dear ~~Santa~~ Mr. Claus ← more respectful
I hope you are well. I am fine.
There really is not very long to go now until Christmas, so I
thought I might write ~~and~~ with a provisional list of presents
in order of preference:

1. A quantity of High Explosive
   (Semtex, or equivalent)
2. Small rubber fork.
3. New mother
4. Brass hook (Toilet door)
5. t.b.a.

December

10.00 Buy New TV

+ Radio Times
TV Times
~~Financial Times~~
TV Quick

QUICK!

NEW ROOM PLANS FOR CHRISTMAS
(TO ACCOMODATE TV)

DOOR

WINDOW

TV

BED

WINDOW

CHAIR

December

17 Friday

CHAIR

DOOR

WINDOW

(LOTS OF SPACE)

WINDOW

BED

18 Saturday

1 Week till

Chizzzy

TV

19 Sunday

CHAIR

DOOR

BRACKET

(EVEN MORE SPACE)

TV

BED

December

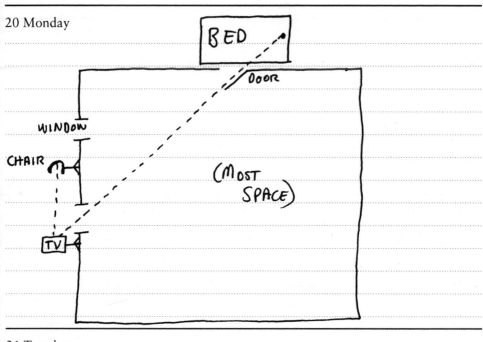

("Daffodils")

Dear Mr. Claus

I hope you are well. I am fine. Only four days till the birthday of our Lord Jesus Christ, and I've had a change of heart: I would now like a Drum Kit which I can bash and bash and bash

New order 1. Snare drum   5. Tom-Tom

2. Cymbal   6. " "

3. Bass drum   7. " "

4. Tom-Tom   8. Brass hook (TOILET DOOR)

4a. Hi-hat   9.

22. Somtesc

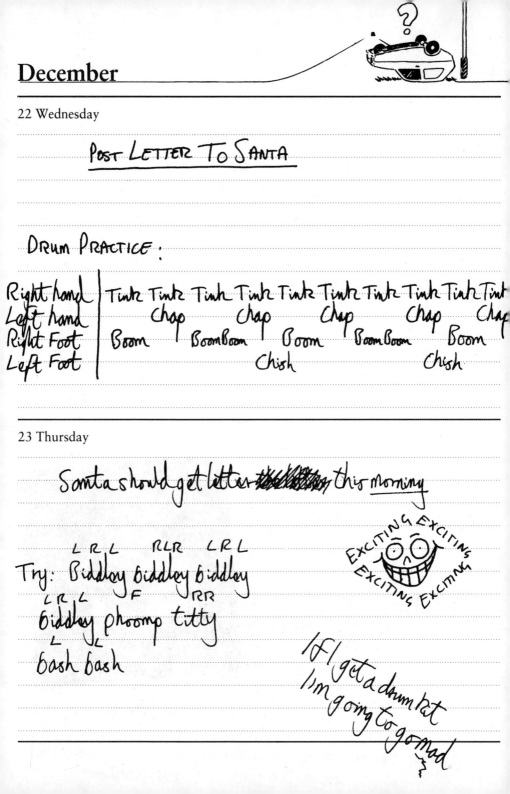

December

22 Wednesday

POST LETTER TO SANTA

DRUM PRACTICE:

Right hand	Tink	Tink	Tink	Tink	Tink	Tink	Tink	Tink	Tink	Tink
Left hand		Chap		Chap		Chap		Chap		Chap
Right Foot	Boom		BoomBoom		Boom		BoomBoom		Boom	
Left Foot				Chish					Chish	

23 Thursday

Santa should get letter ~~this~~ this morning

Try: Biddley Biddley Biddley Biddley phoomp titty bash bash

L R L   R L R   L R L
L R L   F   R R
L   L

EXCITING EXCITING EXCITING EXCITING

If I get a drum kit I'm going to go mad

December

24 Friday

I want a drum kit
I want a drum kit
Tiddle diddle rapple rapple
Bum Boom tish.

Shops: Buy cracker

Buy brass hook.

25 Saturday   Christmas Day

OOOh! BRASS Hook for
Christmas!

Just what I NEED!!

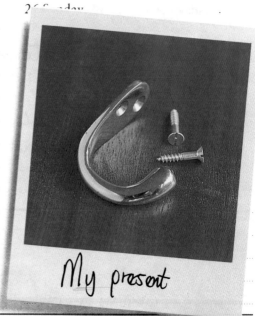

My present

No other presents

(Cracker didn't crack - send back to man)

December

27 Monday   Boxing Day

10.00 Go to Park   (empty)

Practise on
drum kit

No shops open

Evening: stay in

28 Tuesday

Water plant   (in next door garden)

Practise on drum kit

I don't like Christmas very much if I had to be honest

December

29 Wednesday

Practise on drum kit

Shops: Bread
Hazelnut
Tangerine?

---

30 Thursday

9.00 Bird Watching

COMMON WADER

BACK

FRONT

TAKING OFF

SIDE

IN FLIGHT

7.00 Common Wader
(Gas Mark 7
2-2½ hrs.)

31 Friday

New Year Resolutions

1.
2.
3. Tidy room
4.

~~Marriage~~

Can't think of anything

---

1 Saturday

GRAND new YEAR
All clean and sparkling and shiney

1994

GLEAM

SPARKLE

2 Sunday

Nº 3.

Dear Mr Bean,
Would you
like to pop round
for a New Year
drink sometime?
Martin Davis.
(Man in Nº 3.)

P.T.O ⇒

1994 Year Planner

BURY HATCHET

	January	February	March	April	May	June
Mon						
Tue		1	1			
Wed		2	2			1
Thu		3				2
Fri		4				3
Sat	1					4
Sun	2				1	5
Mon	3*				2*	6*
Tue	4*				3	7
Wed	5				4	8
Thu	6				5	9
Fri	7				6	10
Sat	8				7	11
Sun	9				8	12
Mon	10				9	13
Tue	11				10	14
Wed	12				11	15
Thu	13					16
Fri	14					17
Sat	15					18
Sun	16				15	19
Mon	17			18	16	20
Tue	18	22		19	17	21
Wed	19	23	23	20	18	22
Thu	20	24	24	21	19	23
Fri	21	25	25	22	20	24
Sat	22	26	26	23	21	25
Sun	23	27	27	24	22	26
Mon	24	28	28	25	23	27
Tue	25		29	26	24	28
Wed	26		30	27	25	29
Thu	27		31	28	26	30
Fri	28			29	27	
Sat	29			30	28	
Sun	30				29	
Mon	31				30*	
Tue					31	

January	February	March	April	May	June

3 UK, R of Ireland
4 Scotland

17 Ireland (N & R)

1 UK, R of Ireland
4 England, Ireland (N & R), Wales

2 UK
30 UK

6 R of Ireland

1994 Year Planner

	July	August	September	October	November	December
Mon		1*				
Tue		2			1	
Wed		3			2	
Thu		4	1		3	1
Fri	1	5	2		4	2
Sat	2	6	3	1	5	3
Sun	3	7	4	2	6	4
Mon	4	8	5	3	7	5
Tue	5	9	6	4	8	6
Wed	6	10	7	5	9	7
Thu	7	11	8	6	10	8
Fri	8	12	9	7	11	9
Sat	9	13	10	8	12	10
Sun	10	14	11	9	13	11
Mon	11	15	12	10	14	12
Tue	12*	16	13	11	15	13
Wed	13	17	14	12	16	14
Thu	14	18	15	13	17	15
Fri	15	19	16	14	18	16
Sat	16	20	17 *10.00 Sex	15	19	17
Sun	17	21	18 *Change?	16	20	18
Mon	18	22	19 *(Dr. Lahote)	17	21	19
Tue	19	23	20	18	22	20
Wed	20	24	21	19	23	21
Thu	21	25	22	20	24	22
Fri	22	26	23	21	25	23
Sat	23	27	24	22	26	24
Sun	24	28	25	23	27	25
Mon	25	29*	26	24	28	26*
Tue	26	30	27	25	29	27*
Wed	27	31	28	26	30	28
Thu	28		29	27		29
Fri	29		30	28		30
Sat	30			29		31
Sun	31			30		
Mon				31*		
Tue						

July	August	September	October	November	December

12 N Ireland | 1 R of Ireland, Scotland | | 3 R of Irelland | | 26 UK, R of Ireland
 | 29 England, N Ireland Wales | | | | 27 UK, R of Ireland

← CLUE.

Notes

HANGMAN

? ? ?

HAT ×
COT ×
PAT ×
MOT ×
TOM ×
TAM ×
SAP ×
LAP ×
NAP ×
TAP ×
NAP ×
LAP ×
RAT ×
NUT ×
PUT ×
MUT ×
ROP ×
COP ×

PIT × NO
SOP ×
SOAP NO
TOP ×
MOP ×
LOP ×

HOP ×
HELP
NAP ×
MIT ×
MAT ×
CAT ✓

Chadwell School for Boys

Term: SUMMER TERM, 1971 Name: ▓▓▓ EAN

Subject	Mark	Comments	
History	35%	He has no sense of history. But then, of course, he has no sense.	T.A.P.K
Chemistry	53%	He is inventive. As a result, form 5B is lucky to be alive.	T.A.B
Mathematics	96%	An obnoxious, self-satisfied, self-centred, shabby, dribbling, bone-idle, toadying cow-pat of a pupil; his most revolting quality being that he is quite, quite brilliant.	M.J.L.
Physics	65%	Very encouraging. A boy died when co-operating with his lie-detector experiment, as you know, Mr Hu but nevertheless the exam results are excellent.	Mr Hu
Geography	54%	A surprisingly good result considering he only succeeded in finding the classroom twice this term	K.W.
Biology	41%	He really has no idea, but then hopefully he will never breed.	P.A.B
Religious Knowledge	25%	No progress this year, sadly. He once claimed that he worshipped the God of Lemonade which rather confused us all, I'm afraid.	N.N
Art	58%	He draws well, but has difficulty with nudes (looking at them).	P.B.

Good luck. He'll need it. S Love

Headmaster

© Mr. Bean 1993

Notes

PLAN

→ 1. Photocopy this × 10 million

(Joan's CopyShop
10 Slip St.)

then 2.

it.

Graph

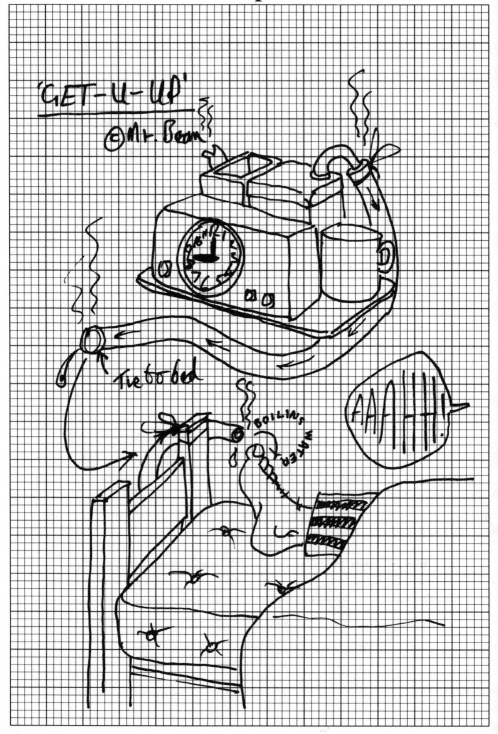

Graph